Contents

KB103012

birthday flower house money picture wood buy could use old if why

A Listen and repeat.   **B** Read, trace, and write.   T1

1. birthday

2. flower

3. house

4. money

5. picture

6. wood

7. buy   buy

8. could   could

9. use   use

10. old   old

11. if   if

12. why   why

C Read and count.

wood   could   money
money
money
could   could
could
wood   wood   money

money ☐

wood ☐

could ☐

D Listen and number.   E Listen, point, and read.

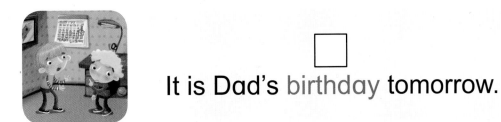

☐

It is Dad's birthday tomorrow.

☐

Ryan uses clay to decorate the frame.

☐

Ryan puts his picture in the frame.

☐   ☐

Friends and family come to Ryan's house.

What Can I Make?

"Ryan, you look sad. Why are you sad?"

"It is Dad's birthday tomorrow.

I don't have any money. If I had some money, I could buy him a nice present."

"You can make him a nice present."

"I can make him a present?

I never thought of that. What can I make?"

Ryan decides to make Dad a nice picture frame.

He uses an old wood frame.

Ryan uses clay to decorate the frame.

He adds flowers on it.

Ryan puts his picture in the frame.

He makes a nice birthday card, too.

They are special because Ryan made them himself. He puts the picture frame and the card in a box.

It is Dad's birthday today.

Friends and family come to Ryan's house.

Ryan gives Dad the present.

Dad opens his present and gives Ryan a big hug.

Activities

A Write, match, and read.

1.

2.

3.

4.

birth ☐☐☐

ho ☐☐☐

pic ☐☐☐☐

flow ☐☐

·   ·   ·   ·

·   ·   ·   ·

use   er   ture   day

B Read, circle, and write.

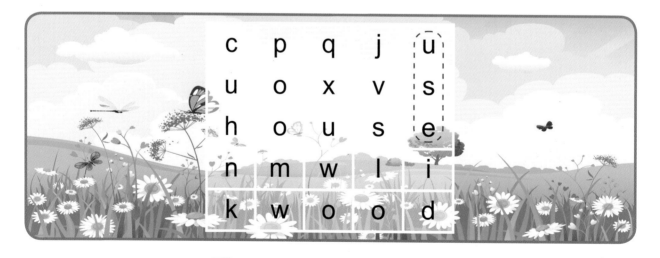

c	p	q	j	u
u	o	x	v	s
h	o	u	s	e
n	m	w	l	i
k	w	o	o	d

1. use _____

2. wood _____

3. house _____

4. could _____

C Fill in the blanks and find a word.

1.

2.

3.

4.

5.

= _____

D Place the stickers and write. 1

1.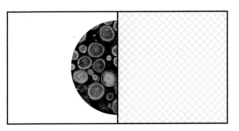

_____

2.

_____

E Listen, repeat and check three times.

F Read on your own and check 😊 or ☹ .

Can you read?

1. birthday ☐☐☐   It is Dad's birthday tomorrow.   😊 ☹

2. if ☐☐☐   If I had some money, I could buy him a nice present.   😊 ☹

3. present ☐☐☐   You can make him a nice present.   😊 ☹

4. can ☐☐☐   What can I make?   😊 ☹

5. picture ☐☐☐   Ryan decides to make Dad a nice picture frame.   😊 ☹

6. use ☐☐☐   Ryan uses clay to decorate the frame.   😊 ☹

7. his ☐☐☐   Ryan puts his picture in the frame.   😊 ☹

8. card ☐☐☐   He puts the picture frame and the card in a box.   😊 ☹

9. house ☐☐☐   Friends and family come to Ryan's house.   😊 ☹

10. open ☐☐☐   Dad opens his present and gives Ryan a big hug.   😊 ☹

G Look, read, and stick. ❷

1.

It is Dad's _____ tomorrow.

2.

What _____ I make?

3.

Ryan decides to make Dad a nice _____ frame.

4.

He puts the picture frame and the _____ in a box.

5.

Friends and family come to Ryan's _____ .

6.

Dad _____ s his present and gives Ryan a big hug.

Words

bell Christmas floor girl Santa toy
run help made down kind new

A Listen and repeat.

B Read, trace, and write.

1.

bell
_____

2.

Christmas
_____

3.

floor
_____

4.

girl
_____

5.

Santa
_____

6.

toy
_____

7.

run
_____

8.
help
help
_____

9.
made
made
_____

10.
down
down
_____

11.
kind
kind
_____

12.
new
new
_____

C Look and draw.

run   made   run   run
made   made
help   made   help   help
run

run = ○

help = △

made = ☐

D Listen and number.

E Listen, point, and read.

☐

"Cindy, try to be kind to other people!"

☐   ☐ ☐

Cindy made up her mind to be a new girl.

☐   ☐

Cindy runs to May to help her up.

☐

It is Christmas morning!

Whole New Cindy

Christmas is coming.

Santa did not give Cindy a present last year.

Santa left a letter instead.

"Cindy, try to be kind to other people!"

Cindy was very sad, and she cried.

Cindy made up her mind to be a new girl.

Last year, Cindy did not share her toys with Mike.

Now, Cindy shares her toys with Mike.

May falls down on the floor.

Cindy runs to May to help her up.

Mrs. Bell is carrying a heavy bag.

Cindy helps her with the heavy bag.

Cindy started this to get Christmas presents. However, now she is kind to others, and that makes her happy.

It is Christmas morning!

Cindy runs to the Christmas tree nervously.

There is a BIG box for Cindy.

Cindy is so excited to open the box.

"Dear Cindy, I am so proud of you!
You are a kind girl now!"

Activities

A Connect, trace, and write.

1.
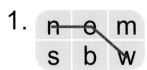
new _____

2.
k c l l
b e d v
bell _____

3.
y a b e
m g d z
made _____

4.
p q n n
d o w v
down _____

B Fill in the blanks and write a word.

1.

2.

3.

 Cindy, I am so proud of ⬡ ▰ ▲ !

C Listen, circle, and write.

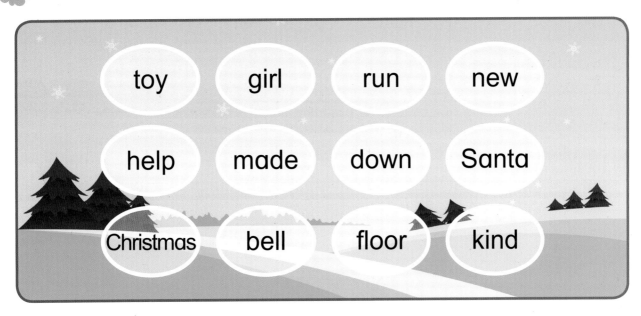

toy   girl   run   new

help   made   down   Santa

Christmas   bell   floor   kind

1. "Cindy, try to be _____ to other people!"

2. Cindy made up her mind to be a new _____.

3. Cindy _____ s her with the heavy bag.

D Read and place the stickers.

1. Now, Cindy shares her _____ s with Mike.

2. Cindy _____ s to May to help her up.

3. It is _____ morning!

E Listen, repeat and check three times.

F Read on your own and check 😊 or ☹️.

Can you read?

1. Santa | ☐☐☐

Santa did not give Cindy a present last year.

😊 ☹️

2. kind | ☐☐☐

"Cindy, try to be kind to other people!"

😊 ☹️

3. made | ☐☐☐

Cindy made up her mind to be a new girl.

😊 ☹️

4. toy | ☐☐☐

Now, Cindy shares her toys with Mike.

😊 ☹️

5. run | ☐☐☐

Cindy runs to May to help her up.

😊 ☹️

6. help | ☐☐☐

Cindy helps her with the heavy bag.

😊 ☹️

7. that | ☐☐☐

She is kind to others, and that makes her happy.

😊 ☹️

8. Christmas | ☐☐☐

It is Christmas morning!

😊 ☹️

9. for | ☐☐☐

There is a big box for Cindy.

😊 ☹️

10. so | ☐☐☐

"Dear Cindy, I am so proud of you!"

😊 ☹️

G **Read and place the stickers. Write the words.** 2

Dear Cindy,

I did not give you a present last year.

You were very sad, and you cried.

You ___1.___ up your mind to be a ___2.___ girl.

You are ___3.___ to others, and that makes you

happy.

I am so proud of you!

You are a kind ___4.___ now!

Love,
Santa

1. _____ _____ _____

2. _____ _____ _____

3. _____ _____ _____

4. _____ _____ _____

eye feet hand head leg street
jump walk hurt try work once

A **Listen and repeat.** **B** **Read, trace, and write.** T9

1.
eye

2.
feet

3.
hand

4.
head

5.
leg

6.
street

7.
jump

8.
walk

9.
hurt
hurt

10.
try
try

11.
work
work

12.
once
once

C Find, match the color, and write.

try jump try try walk
jump walk try walk jump walk

try	walk	jump
try		

D Listen and number. E Listen, point, and read.

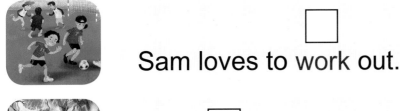 ☐ Sam loves to work out.

 ☐ Sam walks the dog every evening.

 ☐ Bend your head forward and to the back.

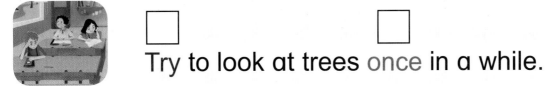 ☐   ☐ Try to look at trees once in a while.

Sam Is in Good Shape

T10

Sam loves to work out.

He exercises every day.

Sam lifts dumbbells every day.

His arms get strong.

Sam stretches every morning.
"Hold your hands together!
Bend to your left and bend to your right."

Sam jumps rope with a friend every afternoon.
His feet and legs hurt, but they get strong.

Sam walks the dog every evening.

Sam and his dog, Shine, walk around the street.

Sam rides a bike once a week.

His legs get strong.

Sam swims twice a week.

His legs and arms get strong.

Sam learns from his coach.

"Bend your head forward and to the back.

This exercise makes your neck stronger."

"Try to look at trees once in a while.
Exercising your eyes makes your vision stronger."

"Keep exercising and you will be strong.
Watch what you eat to stay healthy."

Activities

T11

 A **Write, match, and read.**

1.

2.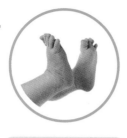

3.

4.

h ☐☐☐   f ☐☐☐   h ☐☐☐   e ☐☐

•   •   •   •

•   •   •   •

eet   ye   and   ead

 B **Look and write.**

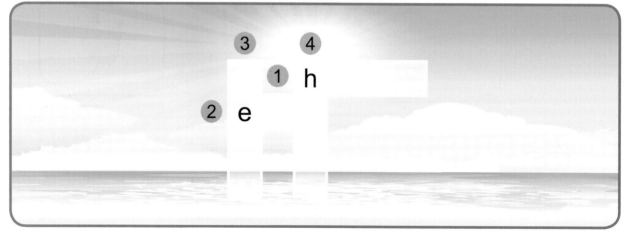

Across →

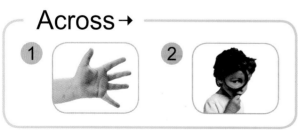

Down ↓

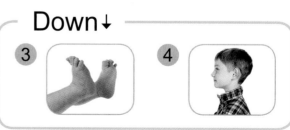

C Fill in the blanks and find a word.

1.

2.

3.

4.

= _____

D Place the stickers and circle. ❶

1. | | | r | k |

    work   head

2. | h | | |

    hurt   work

3. | | | e |

    try   once

4. | s | t | |

    jump   street

E Listen, repeat and check three times.

F Read on your own and check 😊 or ☹ .

Can you read?

1. work ☐☐☐   Sam loves to work out.

2. lift ☐☐☐   Sam lifts dumbbells every day.

3. every ☐☐☐   Sam stretches every morning.

4. jump ☐☐☐   Sam jumps rope with a friend every afternoon.

5. walk ☐☐☐   Sam walks the dog every evening.

6. once ☐☐☐   Sam rides a bike once a week.

7. swim ☐☐☐   Sam swims twice a week.

8. head ☐☐☐   Bend your head forward and to the back.

9. try ☐☐☐   Try to look at trees once in a while.

10. watch ☐☐☐   Watch what you eat to stay healthy.

G Look, follow, and write.

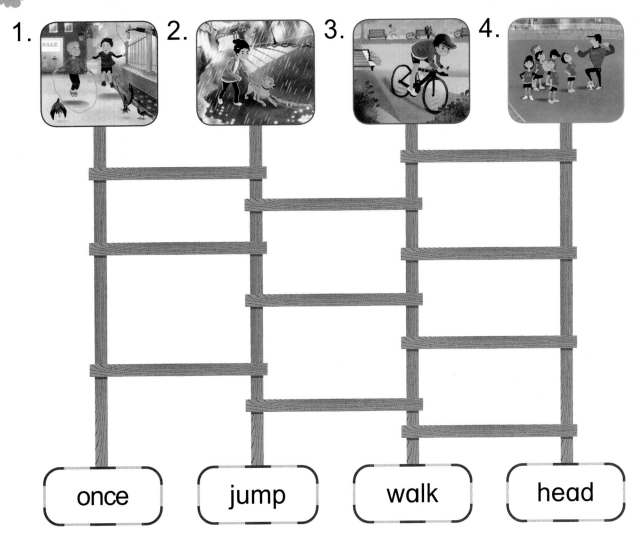

1. Sam _____ s rope with a friend every afternoon.

2. Sam _____ s the dog every evening.

3. Sam rides a bike _____ a week.

4. Bend your _____ forward and to the back.

Unit 4 Words

A Listen and repeat.   **B** Read, trace, and write.

 T13

1.

chicken
_____

2.

cow
_____

3.

farm
_____

4.

sheep
_____

5.

squirrel
_____

6.

table
_____

7.
are
are
_____

8.
be
be
_____

9.
live
live
_____

10.
more
more
_____

11.
in
in
_____

12.
of
of
_____

C Find, circle, and count.

1. in   akineidnfurinmtigjinhkyino ☐

2. of   wieofodjrufofntmgkofhyofa ☐

3. cow   xcowpfoeidhrjtiykcowuonm ☐

4. more qpfmoerymorebrwigmorejrk ☐

D Listen and number.   **E** Listen, point, and read.

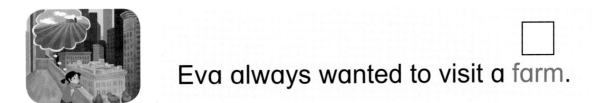

Eva always wanted to visit a farm. ☐

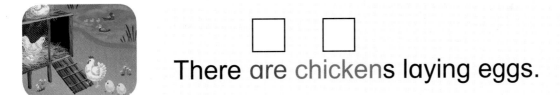

There are chickens laying eggs. ☐ ☐

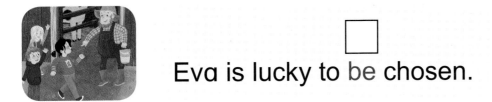

Eva is lucky to be chosen. ☐

A huge table is full of delicious dishes! ☐ ☐

A Field Trip to a Farm

Eva lives in a city.

Eva always wanted to visit a farm.

Eva wakes up early in the morning.

Her class is going on a field trip to a farm today.

They gather at school and get on the bus.

Everyone is excited to go on a field trip.

Eva enjoys the beautiful scenery at the farm.
Beautiful flowers are in the garden.

There are ducks swimming in a pond.
There are chickens laying eggs.

There are sheep grazing on the grass.
There are also cows grazing in the field.

Look at the squirrels climbing the trees.

Pigs are asking for more food saying,

"Oink oink!"

Mr. Green, the farmer, says, "It is time to milk the cow. Are there any volunteers to join me?"

All the children raise their hands saying, "Me!"
Eva is lucky to be chosen.

Now it is everyone's favorite time, lunch time!

A huge table is full of delicious dishes!

Activities

A Connect, trace, and write.

1.
c	x	w
d	o	g

cow _____

2.
m	u	r	e
n	o	n	a

more _____

3.
s	h	o	e	l
c	k	e	o	p

sheep _____

B Fill in the blanks and write a word.

1.

2.

3.

4.

It is _____ to milk the cow.

C Read and draw.

be = △	are = ○	more = □	live = ☆

are	be	are	more
more	live	be	live
be	are	live	more
are	more	are	live

D Listen, circle, and place the stickers. ①

1.
farm	table

fa	

2. live   more

mo	

3.
table	squirrel

	le

4. chicken   sheep

	ep

E Listen, repeat and check three times.

F Read on your own and check 😊 or 🙁 .

Can you read?

1. farm ☐☐☐ Eva always wanted to visit a farm. 😊 🙁

2. field ☐☐☐ Her class is going on a field trip to a farm today. 😊 🙁

3. get ☐☐☐ They gather at school and get on the bus. 😊 🙁

4. beautiful ☐☐☐ Eva enjoys the beautiful scenery at the farm. 😊 🙁

5. chicken ☐☐☐ There are chickens laying eggs. 😊 🙁

6. sheep ☐☐☐ There are sheep grazing on the grass. 😊 🙁

7. squirrel ☐☐☐ Look at the squirrels climbing the trees. 😊 🙁

8. cow ☐☐☐ "It is time to milk the cow." 😊 🙁

9. be ☐☐☐ Eva is lucky to be chosen. 😊 🙁

10. table ☐☐☐ A huge table is full of delicious dishes! 😊 🙁

G Look, number, and stick. ❷

"It is time to milk the _____."

There are _____s laying eggs.

Look at the _____s climbing the trees.

Eva always wanted to visit a _____.

A huge _____ is full of delicious dishes!

Eva is lucky to _____ chosen.

 Review

 Check the words you can read.

- [ ] are
- [ ] be
- [ ] bell
- [ ] birthday
- [ ] buy
- [ ] chicken
- [ ] Christmas
- [ ] could
- [ ] cow
- [ ] down
- [ ] eye
- [ ] farm

- [ ] feet
- [ ] floor
- [ ] flower
- [ ] girl
- [ ] hand
- [ ] head
- [ ] help
- [ ] house
- [ ] hurt
- [ ] if
- [ ] in
- [ ] jump

- [ ] kind
- [ ] leg
- [ ] live
- [ ] made
- [ ] money
- [ ] more
- [ ] new
- [ ] of
- [ ] old
- [ ] once
- [ ] picture
- [ ] run

- [ ] Santa
- [ ] sheep
- [ ] squirrel
- [ ] street
- [ ] table
- [ ] toy
- [ ] try
- [ ] use
- [ ] walk
- [ ] why
- [ ] wood
- [ ] work

Help find the way to his bookshelf.

Write each word on the line.

_____ _____ _____

67

Answer Key

Unit 1

p. 3

C money - 4, wood - 3, could - 3

D

3 It is Dad's birthday tomorrow.

4 Ryan uses clay to decorate the frame.

1 Ryan puts his picture in the frame.

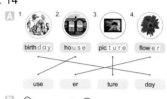
2 5 Friends and family come to Ryan's house.

p. 14

A 1. birth d a y 2. house 3. pic t u re 4. flow e r

use   er   ture   day

B
```
c p q j u
u o x v s
h o u s e
n m w l i
k w o o d
```

p. 15

C 1. picture 2. money 3. house 4. flower 5. birthday

c o u l d = could

D 1. wood — wood 2. house — house

p. 17

G 1. It is Dad's birthday tomorrow.
2. What can I make?
3. Ryan decides to make Dad a nice picture frame.
4. He puts the picture frame and the card in a box.
5. Friends and family come to Ryan's house.
6. Dad opens his present and gives Ryan a big hug.

Unit 2

p. 19

C
run = ○
help = △
made = □

D
4 "Cindy, try to be kind to other people!"
1 Cindy made up her mind to be a new girl.
3 5
2 6 Cindy runs to May to help her up.

7 It is Christmas morning!

p. 30

A 1. n e m / s b w 2. k c l / b e d v 3. y a b e / m g d z 4. p q n n / d o w v

B 1. toy 2. floor 3. run

Cindy, I am so proud of y o u !

p. 31

C
toy (girl) run new
(help) made down Santa
Christmas bell floor (kind)

1. "Cindy, try to be kind to other people!"
2. Cindy made up her mind to be a new girl.
3. Cindy help s her with the heavy bag.

D 1. Now, Cindy shares her toy s with Mike.
2. Cindy run s to May to help her up.
3. It is Christmas morning!

p. 33

G 1. made 2. new 3. kind 4. girl

Unit 3

p. 35

C
try walk jump
walk jump
try walk jump
try
try jump
try walk

D
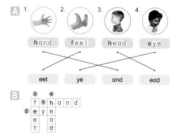
5 Sam loves to work out.
1 Sam walks the dog every evening.
3 Bend your head forward and to the back.
2 4 Try to look at trees once in a while.

p. 46

A 1. hand 2. feet 3. head 4. eye

eet   ye   and   ead

B
```
3 4
f h a n d
2 e y e
e a
t d
```

p. 47

C 1. hand 2. jump 3. street 4. feet

h u r t = hurt

D
1. w o r k (work) head
2. h u r t (hurt) work
3. o n c e try (once)
4. s t r e e t jump (street)

p. 49

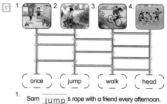

once   jump   walk   head

1. Sam jump s rope with a friend every afternoon.
2. Sam walk s the dog every evening.
3. Sam rides a bike once a week.
4. Bend your head forward and to the back.

Unit 4

p. 51

C
1. in a k t n e i d n f u r i j m t i g i h k y n o 4
2. of w i e o d j r u r o j t m g k o r h y o i a 4
3. cow x c o w o f o e i d h r j t i y k c o w u o n m 2
4. more q p f m o e r y m o r e b r w i g m o r e j r k 2

D
1 Eva always wanted to visit a farm.
3 6 There are chickens laying eggs.
2 Eva is lucky to be chosen.
4 5 A huge table is full of delicious dishes!

p. 62

A 1. c x w / d e g 2. m u r e / n e n a 3. s h o o l / c k e o p

B 1. table 2. chicken 3. farm 4. squirrel

It is t i m e to milk the cow.

p. 63

C be = △ are = ○ more = □ live = ☆
```
are  be  are  more
more (live) be (live)
be  are (live) more
are  more  are (live)
```

D
1. (farm) table 2. live (more)
fa rm   mo re
3. (table) squirrel 4. chicken (sheep)
tab le   she ep

p. 65

G 4 - "It is time to milk the cow."
2 - There are chicken s laying eggs.
3 - Look at the squirrel s climbing the trees.
1 - Eva always wanted to visit a farm.
6 - A huge table is full of delicious dishes!
5 - Eva is lucky to be chosen.

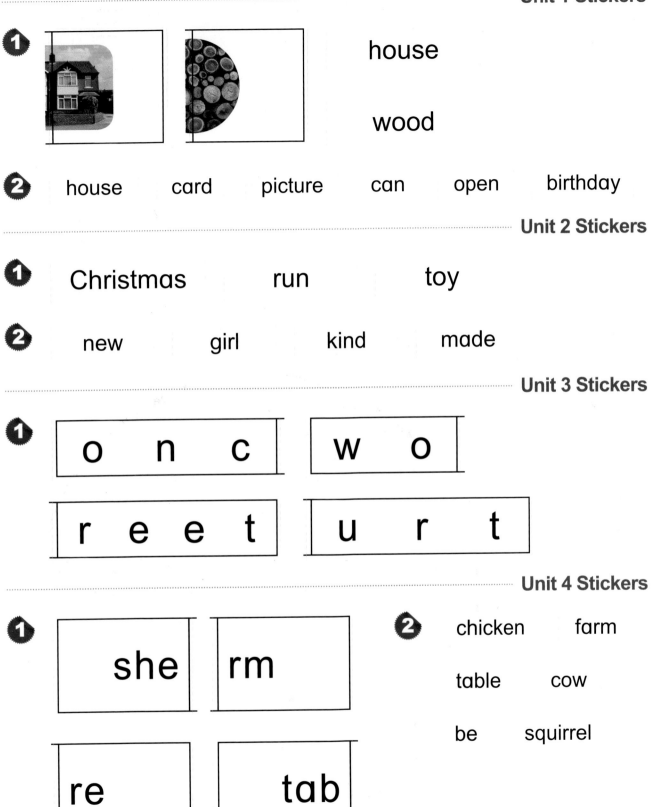

1 house

wood

2 house   card   picture   can   open   birthday

1 Christmas   run   toy

2 new   girl   kind   made

1

| o | n | c |

| w | o |

| r | e | e | t |

| u | r | t |

1

she   rm

re   tab

2 chicken   farm

table   cow

be   squirrel